Travelpedia

A Quick Guide on How to Travel Efficiently, Healthy and Safely

Travelpedia

A Quick Guide on How to Travel Efficiently, Healthy and Safely

Yvette McQueen, MD

TRAVELPEDIA

Published by Purposely Created Publishing Group™

Copyright © 2018 Yvette McQueen

All rights reserved.

Printed in the United States of America

ISBN: 978-1-948400-94-7

Special discounts are available on bulk quantity purchases by book clubs, associations and special interest groups. For details email: sales@publishyourgift.com or call (888) 949-6228.

For information log on to www.PublishYourGift.com

Dedication

I dedicate this book to my family:

My mother, Mary V McQueen. She has been my guiding force to exploring my mind's potential, the one who encouraged me to reach for my dreams wherever they take me.

My father, Josh McQueen. He organized my first international trip.

My sisters, Ethlyn Gibson and Teresa Thompson. They are the most wonderful big sisters ever. They fostered my adventurous spirit and supported my unconventional imagination. And they trusted me to be the "other mother" to their children.

My nieces and nephews who have tolerated their free spirit Auntie.

Colton and Emerson Hubbard, who will one day read this and know I love them.

I also would like to dedicate this book to Ray, Mike, and all the airport personnel who have assisted me in my travels over the past years; and most importantly, helped me not to miss my flights.

Table of Contents

Foreword

When I consider where my passion and quest for exploration comes from, all roads lead back to Yvette McQueen, MD.

In July 1980, I was blessed to come into this world and to be surrounded by a group of very strong black women: my mother, grandmother, and aunts. Yvette, who was 16 years old at the time of my birth, is not only my aunt but also like a mother to me. She was my very first friend and, even today, she is absolutely my best friend, mentor, role model, and a constant source of support.

Over the course of my lifelong relationship with Yvette, I have learned so many things. Our bond has sustained me as I have progressed through this journey of life, through my most personal self-explorations and the highs and lows that inevitably come with interactions with external exploration. From our relationship, I have come to learn, understand, and embrace my value and the right that I have to experience joy, curiosity, wonder, and delight in life. This willingness to accept such a right has come through my observations of Yvette and her love for not only travel, but also the way she couples that love with the passion she has for her medical career, along with the love and commitment she shows to all the ones who she loves around her.

Stagnancy and complacency are the antithesis of the foundation of the true Yvette McQueen MD. From the very early moment of her life until today, Yvette has been willing to push the boundaries and barriers that somehow limit others in their lives. Yvette's love for travel and exploration is the source of inspiration for this book, but it is a part of the soundtrack of her life and her commitment to the service of others.

For Yvette, travel has connected her to some of the furthest corners of the world, but it has also fostered her love, care, and desire to nurture humanity in an effort to make the world a better place through health, wellness, and a desire to explore the unseen and unknown. This book allows us to see our own travels through her lens and passion for travel, exploration, wonder, curiosity, and delight. May this book unlock the desire for not only travel but for self exploration and discovery in your life, and inspire you to use that journey to make our world a better place.

Faith Gibson Hubbard, PhD

Introduction

Ever since I was a child I have traveled, and I always thought everyone else traveled just as much as me. My middle class, modest income, Midwest family traveled! We would pile into the station wagon and travel for holidays. We always took a family vacation in August before school started. And through school, I traveled to places like Niagara Falls, the state capitol, Amish country, and the nation's capital Washington DC.

Our family owned a set of World Book Encyclopedias. I would look at the shiny, colored pictures of places and countries and dream of visiting them. In middle school, I signed up in a Pen Pal program and regularly wrote to a girl in West Germany. Fast forward to high school, my parents gifted me with a trip to visit her in Germany. I got my first passport at the age of 14. And once I went international, I haven't stopped.

That's why it's amazing to me when people tell me today that they have never traveled outside of the United States and do not own a passport. Some people have never even crossed the Mississippi River or traveled to the opposite coast in our very own country. I am constantly asked about how to start traveling and have helped others plan many first-time international trips. So, I wrote this book is to help anyone and everyone who wants to travel; it will help you plan your trip and push past the fear of traveling. I will also offer guidelines to traveling efficiently, healthy, and safely.

Go from couch dweller to explorer. Live your dream!

CHAPTER 1

Why I Travel

EXPLORER: one that explores; especially a person who travels in search of geographical or scientific information; a person who explores an unfamiliar area; an adventurer.

synonyms: traveler, discoverer, voyager, adventurer, surveyor, scout, prospector

(www.merriam-webster.com/dictionary/explorer)

I travel because I am an explorer. I travel to gain knowledge of culture, history, and people; and along the way I find pleasure in my surroundings.

People travel for various reasons: vacation, adventure, family, business, education, fact-finding, bucket list, spiritual soul-searching, or just to wander.

> **WANDERLUST:** a strong, innate desire to rove or travel about.
> *(www.dictionary.com)*

I have traveled for all the above reasons, but the planning stages are always the same. Organization is a key element for a smooth transition. And even when you have crossed off the list and ticked off all the boxes, "life" can change the timeline at any point.

You may decide to travel solo and enjoy the solitude; not depending on anyone else's schedule. The drawback is that on certain vacations such as cruises or tours, you may have to pay extra as a single supplement. The travel industry believes it takes more effort to serve one person than two people. Hmm....

Or you may travel with a small group: families, friends, couple's trips, girls' getaways, guys' trips, clubs, etc. Coordination between people, schedules, and preferences will be limiting factors.

Group travel is the new and exciting experience for the solo traveler. Group travel consists of an organized trip in which you purchase. All of the travel, lodging, and activities are preplanned; all you have to do is pay, show up, and have fun. Groups are typically 10 or more people, a diverse assembly of people you may not know before the trip. The explosion of travel groups on social media has encouraged many who thought they could never travel to go on an adventure. Group travel works well for solo travelers: you can join the group, sign up for a trip, and get assigned a roommate. Nix the single supplement! In fact, group travel has become increasingly economical since most groups offer payment plans 8 to 24 months prior to the trip. Imagine paying $50 a month for a trip of the lifetime.

You can also find a group that's just right for you. Groups vary in their complexity: some have single organizers who bring people together but have no planned events while others are organized and guided from beginning to end. Some groups cater to luxury experiences, adventures, explorations, etc. There are also travel groups that cater to different demographics and types of people: young, over 50, women only, singles, couples, LGBTQ, and more. Choose one for your taste.

I have been a traveling physician for a few travel groups to offer pre-travel information and medical care while traveling. I enjoy the interaction with other travelers, their diverse viewpoints, and the comradery on excursions. And the extra perks and group swag bags are a special touch.

Chapter 2

From Couch Dweller to Explorer: How to Get Started

What are your fears of travel? Not enough money? Afraid of traveling alone? Worried about traveling outside of the US and safety? Leary of hotels? Some people tell me they are afraid of not enjoying their vacation after paying the money, going somewhere unknown, traveling outside of the US will be dangerous, or getting sick while on vacation. Others fear the stress of planning and going on vacation only to return more stressed.

Whatever your fears, know that they will keep you trapped on your couch while the world keeps turning. The fears will remain there until you leap, or more appropriately, roll off the couch, pack a bag, and walk out the door. Aristotle said, "Courage is the first of human virtues because it makes all others possible."

So how do you go from your couch to becoming an explorer? First, you should acknowledge your fear of traveling. Are your fears rational and grounded in facts? We base our knowledge of the unknown on another person's poor understanding and bad experiences. Imagine two people watching a movie and they leave the theater with opposite opinions.

Second, embrace your vulnerabilities. You deserve to see and experience new people, cultures, and destinations, but you must get comfortable with being uncomfortable as you travel to new places and encounter new methods of being and living. Accept that no vacation will be perfect: there will be delay and changes, and you won't always be in control of your schedule unless you are the driver or pilot. Remember to be flexible and adaptable. Also, put away the cynicism particularly when you leave the US; you are no longer in the USA and people live differently than us. And just because it's different does not mean it is the wrong way. Learn from these moments.

And third, actively expose yourself to your fear. What are your limitations? You don't have the expenses, time, or courage to leave the country. Then visit a neighboring state or even a city on the other side of the state. Or discover a national park or monument that's close by to explore. Just do it!

Take action with a specific plan. The next three-day weekend or holiday, pack a bag and leave your house. You may hear people complain how the family vacation was stressful. A vacation can also be the answer to your everyday stress; remove yourself from daily activities, sleep late, have someone else cook your meals. Turn your fear of traveling into joy.

SO HOW DO YOU GET STARTED?

1. Pick a time: reasonably and within the next 10 months. Why 10 months? It's less than a year and achievable; not too close to be worried about reservations, but far enough that you can save and make payments for the trip.

2. Select the length of your trip: I suggest four to seven days. Three days is too short because time for getting to your destination is a factor. You will only be able to enjoy the destination two days and you'll feel rushed to enjoy everything at once. Four days is the time typically needed

to adjust to fluctuations of weather, time zones, or any other changes. More than seven days may interfere with your work or family obligations; and as a first-time traveler, you are ready to return home.

3. Choose your pleasure: hiking, adventurous quests, historical tours, change of weather, beach, skiing, relaxation, food discoveries, wine tasting experiences. Whatever passion that brings you joy. There are destinations for all desires.

4. Determine a budget: decide on the amount of money you want to spend on yourself and never see again. While this may invoke an uneasy feeling, this investment is in your sanity, well-being, and positive emotions. The return in investment will be an enhanced self-confidence of your achievement.

5. Decide where to go: All the above decisions will dictate where you choose as your destination. Do you want to stay local? Same state? A neighboring state? Across the country? Outside the country? Researching your destination is advised to discover lodging, transportation, activities, weather, culture, food availability, and more.

6. Lodging: Today, we have many options other than a hotel. Many people offer up their houses, apartments, and condos for rent through

Airbnb, vacation rental by owner (VRBO), Hometogo, and many other new housing websites. Most places can be reserved online with a credit card deposit unless it's way off the grid. Renting a house can be more cost efficient for large parties over four persons when compared to booking multiple hotel rooms. There are also vacation exchange sites (RCI, Interval World, etc.) for long-forgotten timeshares.

If you prefer the hotel experience, make sure you are a member of the brand's member awards or points program. Even if you don't travel enough to accumulate a free night's stay, they will send you specials and incentives such as "Book 4 nights, get the 5th night free."
Now that you have a general idea of where you want to go, why you want to go there, and where you will be staying, let's talk about transportation.

CHAPTER 3

Modes of Transportation

Whether you are staying within your own state or traveling internationally, there various ways to get your destination. And at times you may use combined modes of transportation; example, a flight to a major city and then a two-hour drive. Here are some of the choices that you have:

AUTOMOBILE: USING YOUR OWN VEHICLE VS. RENTING A CAR

- *Using your own vehicle:* if you are driving to your destination, map out your route ahead of time. You can get maps (printed, downloads, apps) from various sources, some that even provide you up to date traffic conditions and construction on the roads. Determine the maximum amount of time you'll spend on the road including meal times, rest, and gas stops. Cars with navigation or your smart phone's map app will let you know the nearest gas stations on your route, so you can plan accordingly. Finally, before you leave home, make sure that the maintenance on your vehicle is up to date and that you can successfully make the trip. If not, consider car rental for your journey.

- *Renting a vehicle:* You can rent vehicles at an airport, hotel, or rental sites throughout the city. If you rent a car from the airport, you will be charged an airport excess fee; and you will need to factor in the time it takes to shuttle to the car or walk from the airport terminal.

  You can reserve your car in advance and not pay until you pick it up, or you can prepay for a discounted price that is nonrefundable even if you don't use the car. Rental companies will also offer a discount for airline frequent flier programs, AAA, AARP, and other memberships and organizations. A major credit card is necessary to obtain a rental car; if you use your debit card, you will be charged a $200 to $500 hold on your account, which may not be released for 5 to 7 days after you return the car. Basically, they hold your money until they get their property back in good condition. By the way, most car rental companies now only have non-smoking vehicles and will charge a hefty cleaning fee for smoking in the vehicle.

Reserve the class of car that is appropriate for your vacation activity; only upgrade to another class if there is no additional charge and be aware of your gas options. The prepay gas option allows you to pay for a full tank of gas at the current gas price and you can return the car without refueling. If you don't use all of the gas, you are *not* refunded the partial amount; however, if you plan to use the full tank of gas, the prepay gas option can be economical and save you time when you return the car.

You should consider joining the car rental company membership programs to collect points and credits to gain status that can be applied for upgrades and/or free rentals.

OTHER TIPS AND INFORMATION FOR TRAVELING BY AUTOMOBILE:

- Stop every two hours to get up and stretch your legs for at least 10 to 15 minutes to stimulate circulation. Blood clots can form in your legs when you are sedentary for two or more hours. *Do not* try driving for 8 to 12 hours straight without stopping. It is hazardous to your health and to others.

- Keep an emergency kit in your car for unexpected occurrences. Be sure to modify and adapt the kit according to the environment of your travel route: blankets for the cold, shovel and ice scraper for snow, extra clothes and hats for warmth or sun exposure, etc. Other items to keep in the car include bottle water, snacks, flash light with extra batteries, multipurpose utility tool, work gloves, foam tire sealant, jumper cables, rope, white towel/cloth, reflective light sticks, duct tape, sanitizer, and a first aid kit. This is not a comprehensive list and you can add according to your situations.

TRAINS: SCHEDULES AND SYSTEMS

Trains travel on set schedules and typically are on time. However, the train systems vary between different cities, states, and countries; so carefully research the rail system of your destination. In my experience, the Europe rail system is efficient, punctual, and comfortable; but be aware of rail strikes that can disrupt your travel.

OTHER TIPS AND INFORMATION FOR TRAVELING BY TRAIN:

- Trains have different class tickets for your budget: premium, business, coach.

- Most long-distance trains have seating accommodations, meals or meal/dining section, and sleeping accommodations.

- Reserve tickets in advance: be flexible during the holidays and vacation season.

- Discounts are available by age, organizations, memberships, etc. (We'll talk more about international train travel in later chapters.)

- Luggage racks are available on trains. Some trains even offer checked baggage.

- Remember that, even when you reach your train stop, you may still have to travel to your hotel or any other destination.

CHAPTER 4

Traveling by Air

- *Buying your ticket:* You can book an airline ticket online through a specific airline's website, a travel website, an airline or travel app, or with a travel agent. Many online sites will even compare prices for you, so you get the best deal amongst the airlines. You can still call an airline directly and speak with a reservation agent, but there may be an extra fee added to the ticket. By law, the total ticket price including fees or charges must be disclosed prior to your purchase.

If you are able, buy your ticket 14 to 21 days before your departure. Contrary to popular belief, buying your ticket six months in advance does not make it cheaper unless you catch a "sale" with an airline. Occasionally there is a "glitch fare" in which tickets are deeply discounted because of computer or human error. You can set fare watch sites [*see appendix*] to catch these fares. You need to be flexible and spontaneous to take advantage of the glitch fares. Be careful. Most airlines will honor these glitches, but the smaller airlines have been known to cancel the ticket.

Why are airline seats priced differently and change within minutes to hours? Airlines will sell a seat on the same flight under different fare classes (not seat classes). An economy class seat will be labeled from class "B" to "Y" depending on the location of the seat, the time of the flight, or other variables; and these classes of seats vary in costs. So, the person seating next to you could easily have paid $100 less than your ticket. The most cost-effective days to fly are Tuesdays, Wednesdays, and Saturdays. Some discounted fares require 21 days vs. 14 days vs. 7 days in advance; other fares are blacked out or not available around holidays or other peak travel times (Spring Break, summer vacation, etc.).

Once your ticket is purchased, download the app for that airline and store your ticket reservation in your smartphone. Also, be sure to join the airline frequent flier program to accumulate points or miles. Did you know the Department of Transportation requires the airlines to give you a 24-hour grace period to cancel for a full refund for any reason if the flight is 7 days or more?

- *Choose your seat:* If you have the airline's app, you can choose your seats before or at the time of check-in. Airlines will charge for the premium seats like the ones in the exit row or bulk head (wall in front of you or section divider). Airlines will also charge for upgraded seats called "Comfort" seats, which have a few more inches of the leg room; however, be aware that the seats are still narrow. The website seatguru.com helps you find the seat map of airlines and aircrafts; it informs you of seats with conditions such as having limited reclining abilities, no window, or equipment under the seat in front of you which limits your storage.

- *Checking in online:* You can check into your flight 24 hours before departure by app or online. If you have the app on your smartphone, you can use it as your boarding pass to get through TSA and at the departure gate. You can also print out the ticket at home or at the airport but be sure not to lose the piece of paper. If you should lose your printed ticket, you can show your ID, and have it reprinted at an airline help desk, the gate, or a kiosk machine scattered throughout some airports.

- *Arriving at the airport:* First time travelers should arrive at the airport at least two hours before the flight departure. It allows for time to find airport parking if you are leaving your car and other possible delays. If you have extra time, it reduces your stress while standing in line for bag check or security.

- *Checking your bags*: If you are not Elite or Priority status, you may have to stand in a long line to check your bag. To check luggage on a domestic flight, you are charged $25–35 per person for the first bag; higher for any additional luggage. You can pay online when you check in for the flight or at the airline counter with a credit card; cash is *not* accepted. You are not charged for checked luggage on an international flight with most airlines.

If you choose to check your bags outside with the baggage handlers, *PLEASE* tip them at least $2 per bag. They are handling your precious luggage and you want to make sure it starts the journey with you.

- *Getting through TSA security*: You must have a valid federal ID to pass through the TSA, along with your boarding pass (phone or paper). Make sure you have the "REAL ID" driver's license enacted in 2014; some states' licenses are no longer accepted as a federal ID. If you don't have the proper license, you can use a passport or passport card. Some airports have begun accepting your fingerprints through CLEAR as identification.

  Unless you are Pre-Check or CLEAR status, you will need to go through the normal security line. You may have a shorter line if you are Elite or Priority status with an airline, but the same security requirements apply to you.

  You also cannot travel with any liquid or gel items greater than 3.4 ounces; and they must all fit in one quart size bag. Exceptions are baby formula or medications with an approved medical clearance letter (see appendix). If you have any special clearance, notify the agent prior to getting in line. When going through security, you will remove all items from your pockets.

You will also remove all heavy metal, belts, and shoes before going through the detector (wear socks or have slip-on footies to avoid walking on the cold/dirty floor). Take out all laptop computers and place them in a bin all by itself. Do not carry any weapons, scissors, knives or guns. Yes, it needs to be said. You can take food through TSA security, but it must not include any liquids; soups are not allowed. Don't let them confiscate your grand mama's sweet potato pie! *(Please check the up to date TSA rules because they are constantly changing www.tsa.gov/travel.)*

If you are pregnant, always check with your physician for approval to travel by airplane. The cutoff is usually 36 weeks gestation for any air travel. Trust me, delivering a baby at 30,000 feet is not a task any physician wishes. The radiation is minimal going through the security check but, if you wish to bypass it, you can elect to have a security pat-down. Just notify the TSA agent of your choice.

TSA Pre-Check is a security clearance in which you have applied for and gone through a background check to verify your identity. Most frequent fliers and business travelers use this to expedite the process through security. You do not have to remove clothes, belts, shoes, or items from your bags, but you may be still subject to individual search at random. CLEAR is an extra security clearance in which your fingerprints and retina scans are obtained. In some airports, you can bypass all TSA lines with CLEAR but you still have to go through the detectors. You can also use your fingerprints as your boarding pass at the gate.

- *Waiting for your flight:* There are usually shops, restaurants and restrooms near your departure gate. And many airports have charging stations or seats installed with electrical outlets for recharging electronics. You should be at your gate 40 minutes before your flight departure; and many announcements are made only at the gate regarding changes and delays. Once again, the airline app will send you notifications of flight changes. This is a great time for you to buy a bottle of water or refill your reusable water bottle at a water-filling station. Hydration is a necessity during air travel.

An airline club membership is worth the extra cost, particularly for frequent and business travelers. You can relax between flights and enjoy free meals and drinks, free Wi-Fi and printers, clean bathrooms, and even showers in international terminals. There are also nice airline agents to help you change your seat or your flight.

Airline club membership can be a perk of an airline status: Delta Sky Club, United Priority Pass, and American Admiral Club; or obtained by having a particular credit card with Chase or American Express. You can purchase daily passes if you are not a frequent flier and have a long delay in between flights. If you have a yearly membership, your benefits may extend to many international partners' clubs including Air France, KLM, Lufthansa, South African Air etc.

- *Boarding your flight:* You can carry on one personal item (purse, backpack, computer case, instrument, etc.) and one piece of appropriately-sized luggage aboard the plane. Carry-on bags are only supposed to weigh 25 lbs./12 kg, and some international carriers will weigh your bag at the gate. Be careful of extra items because some gate agents will ask you to consolidate them. Food items do not qualify as a personal item; you can bring food and drinks on board if purchased after security. Please board the airplane according to the gate agent's instructions and your correct zone. Crowding around the gate door only delays the boarding and departure. If you are concerned about space for your carry-on luggage, ask the gate agent for a complementary bag check.

AIRPLANE ETIQUETTE:

- Don't sit in another seat, hoping that someone will switch with you. Wait until they board and ask nicely.

- Don't fall asleep on the person next to you and drool on them.

- If your flight has a personal video screen on the back of the seat in front of you, don't punch the screen to change the channel. You are poking someone's back.

- If you have food that smells (tuna, fish, curry, etc.), save it until you are off the plane. It is a closed compartment and smells travel.

- Don't sit in the window seat if you know you will have to go to the bathroom several times during the flight.

- Do not change your baby's diapers on the tray table.

- Do not let your support animal eat off the tray table.

- Don't poke the flight attendant.

- Wear shoes when you enter the bathroom.

- Don't kick the back or underside of the seat in front of you.

CHAPTER 5

When to Travel, Following the Deal, and How to Protect Your Travels

WHEN TO TRAVEL

I'm often asked when is the best time to travel. The answer depends on your destination and purpose. If you're traveling for leisure and relaxation, adjust it according to your schedule. Holidays and the summertime will always be high travel traffic times. The travel industry has low seasons or "shoulder seasons" during which prices may be reduced: January to February (immediately following holidays), March to April before schools are out (but avoid warm and beach areas frequented by spring breakers), and September to October/early November (after children return to school but before the holidays). Although during low season some resorts or destination cities may have reduced availability, activities, or even closed attractions. For example, Gatlinburg stops their shows during February, and Key West businesses close to take vacation during early October. I recommend researching the destination to determine the tourist season and availabilities.

As mentioned previously, travel industry experts recommend off-peak days; there is less demand of flights on Tuesday, Wednesday, and sometimes Saturday. Flights on Mondays, Thursday afternoons, and Fridays are usually filled with business travelers.

FOLLOW THE DEAL

Tuesday night and early Wednesday morning is the best time to purchase an airline ticket. The "why" explanation is a long algorithm that I don't fully understand but it works. Flights are less expensive when they take off early in the morning (before 8:00 am) or late in the evening (after 7:00 pm). Be careful of low budget air carriers. They list lower ticket prices but add fees for everything from carry-on luggage, seat selection, and food.

Several online sites will alert you to flight deals or track the cost of your destination for you, flash sales, last-minute deals, or glitch fares. But you need to be ready: if you see a great deal, it will probably only last for a few hours. If you are an airline frequent flier, the airlines will send out flight sales and last-minute deals to their members first before releasing them to the public. Or follow the airline on Twitter for sale notifications. Some sites will offer deals on vacation packages for flight and hotel combinations (see appendix for online sites to track and deal alerts). You should look for flights at a nearby airport to your destination for a cheaper flight instead of a major hub. Use your memberships and associations (AAA, AARP, schools, clubs, military, professional, etc.) for additional discounts at hotels and car rentals.

If you are overwhelmed by the process of booking your flight, car, hotel, or any other amenities, just use a travel agent. Yes, they still exist. A travel agent does not charge you a fee; they receive commission and perks from the sources you reserve. A travel agent may also have additional incentive credits not available on online sites.

TRAVEL INSURANCE

You book your honeymoon, second honeymoon, trip of a lifetime or a luxury getaway. It's 10 months away and you have a steady payment plan. The tours are organized, your trip is paid, you are ready, and your excitement builds; then life happens.

Travel insurance is an expense that should always be added into the budget. You can buy insurance when you purchase airline tickets and/or book a vacation package. If you are a business traveler or travel more than two international trips per year, you should consider an annual travel insurance policy. It can be bought through the airlines, your credit card company, your travel agent, or independent travel insurance agencies. Policies vary and can compensate events such as delay of travel (you missed a flight and then missed the cruise), delay of bags (greater than six hours), loss of bags, and even cancellation of trip for any reason.

Medical travel insurance is a necessity while traveling internationally. If you become ill or have an accident while traveling, your US-based medical insurance typically will not cover your medical care internationally, but more importantly, most international medical facilities will *not* accept it. Non-US medical facilities will require payment before service in the form of cash or credit card. To be seen in an A&E (Emergency Room) in a foreign country is not as costly as in the US, but it can be a nuisance, timely, and disrupt your vacation. Medical travel insurance is helpful because it can be accepted by international medical facilities or you are reimbursed for your payment upon your return home. You can obtain assistance in finding services nearby for your medical need and, if necessary, you can be evacuated to a higher-level care facility in another country or back to the US. There are different types of medical travel insurance available: one-time vacation, annual traveler, business traveler, adventurer, student abroad, mission traveler, and more. The cost of medical travel insurance is usually dependent on the cost of the trip and the age of the traveler. Medical travel insurance will add a little extra cost to your vacation, but it saves you a large amount of anxiety, frustration, and money, if needed.

CHAPTER 6

Traveling with Infants and Toddlers

Don't worry, don't stress; traveling with children is possible. Either in a car or on an airplane, the key is to keep them active, full and occupied. Sleeping is also an alternative option.

Children under two-years-old fly for free if they are in your lap. The older and more mobile your child becomes, the harder it is to contain them; but you can purchase a ticket for them and bring their car seat or carrier to put in the seat. If flying internationally, your child will need a ticket, even if they are traveling in your lap. Usually, the ticket is 10 percent the cost of the regular ticket. Please call and let the airline agent know you that you will be traveling with a lap infant when you purchase your ticket, so you aren't surprised when you're asked to pay at check-in and then get delayed or miss your flight. If you want to purchase a seat for the international flight, ask for a discounted ticket for children 2 years old and under.

If possible, get a direct flight. If a layover is necessary, arrange for it to be 90 minutes or greater for a smooth transport from gate to gate; and bathroom stops.

When choosing your seats, try to get the bulkhead seat with a wall in front of you. On international flights, the attendants will reserve those seats for people traveling with an infant and they have a bassinet available after takeoff. You can also purchase an airplane lap bassinet for infants.

Children do need passports to travel internationally. You can get them as soon as after birth with a certified birth certificate. You go through the same application process as with adults. However, both parents must give consent for the passport or you must prove that you are the sole parent. The passport is valid for five years. Also, consider obtaining a passport card for your child: you can use it as their federal ID and for age verification.

For smaller infants, a baby carrier that you strap to your body is helpful during transport since it leaves you hands-free. You can take your stroller through security and then check it at the gate. It will be returned to you in the jet-way upon landing. You will need it in the airport for the distance from security to the gate or while walking between connecting flights. The car seat can also be checked with your luggage or at the gate. I suggest getting a cover to protect your stroller or car seat because, when placed in airplane cargo, it can get scratched and dirty. The checked car seat is not counted as checked luggage and you are not charged for it.

A diaper bag can be brought on the plane along with your other two carry-on items. The diaper bag should include 5–7 diapers for the day, baby wipes, bags for dirty diapers, powder or cream, sanitizing wipes, disposable changing pads, bibs, bottle, formula, pacifier in a re-sealable bag, and a change of clothes. A pacifier is great for a child to suck on during takeoffs and landings; it helps with the ear pressure. You can also nurse or give your baby a bottle for the same effect.

Toddlers should bring their favorite toy and book. Toys should not have multiple pieces, and be sure to tie a string on them for the multiple times the child will drop them. The toddler's carry-on bag should include toys, books, food pouches, milk or juice, tissues, a change of clothes, and snacks. A tablet can be loaded with age-appropriate apps, games, books, puzzles, etc. A first aid kit, a thermometer, fever-reducing medication, and a comfortable blanket is useful. Parents should include a change of clothes for themselves in their own carry-on.

FYI: You can save space in your luggage if you buy diapers when you reach your destination (if available). Check with your hotel or lodging about resources for children prior to travel.

CHAPTER 7

Domestic vs. International Travel

WHERE TO TRAVEL

If you don't know where to travel but have your dates and a budget, use Google Flights. It's a user-friendly search market to explore destinations for your parameters. Plug in the city you are leaving from, the travel dates, and your budget. And voila! It will show you travel possibilities all over the world.

DOMESTIC TRAVEL WITHIN THE UNITED STATES

Other than the state you live, you have 49 other states in the United States to explore the majestic valleys, mountains, rivers, beaches, canyons, and so, so much. You don't need a passport; just a desire to explore. Each state has at least one natural wonder, historical site, or national landmark. The 49 states are connected by car, train, and airplane. Yes, you can drive to Alaska! Hawaii is the only state you cannot drive to since it sits in the middle of the Pacific Ocean. I suggest traveling by airplane although a ship is also a mode of transportation to reach the island.

The United States is a vast land with a diverse map. It offers various scenery from large cities, small towns, beaches, farms, etc. It offers activities such as skiing, fishing, hiking, hunting, bird watching, and some I don't even know. Travel across the USA deserves its own book. I will provide a state-by-state dissection in *Volume 2* after I have traveled to all 50 states. I'm close!

INTERNATIONAL TRAVEL

To leave and re-enter the United States, you must have a valid US passport. If you are a naturalized citizen or green card holder, please check the current regulations regarding international travel before purchasing your flight and/or vacation package. International travel includes traveling by ground to the neighboring countries of Canada and Mexico. If traveling by cruise ship to the Caribbean, Bahamas, or Bermuda, you can use a federal ID (driver's license/military ID/State ID) with a picture *and* a birth certificate or a passport card, in case you do not have a passport.

HOW TO GET A PASSPORT

Complete the application from the US State Department website: https://travel.state.gov/content/travel/en/passports/requirements/forms.html

Print the completed form, but do *not* sign it. Then, get a 2x2 passport picture, which can be obtained several places: drugstore photo counter, photographer, photo booth, or post office passport office.

Bring a copy of your federal ID (driver license or state ID) and your original birth certificate or citizenship documents to a US Post Office that has a passport service. You can apply for a passport booklet (typically with pages for entry stamps) and/or passport card, but a passport card can only be used for land or sea travel to Canada, Mexico, Bermuda, and the Caribbean. The fees must be paid with check or money order.

The process typically takes 4–6 weeks. You can use a passport agency to process your application for an additional fee; and a passport can be expedited if you need it in less than 4 weeks with an additional fee. If you need a passport in less than a week, you can make an appointment at a passport agency via this website (https://travel.state.gov/content/travel/en/passports/requirements/where-to-apply/passport-agencies.html), but be prepared to show proof of immediate international travel. The passport is valid for 10 years.

ENTERING A FOREIGN COUNTRY

Some countries require a VISA for entry into their country. Check with the US State Department or the country's website to determine if the visa can be obtained upon entry of the country (which can be time consuming upon arrival) or if it is required prior to travel. If prior to travel, you must file an application to the country's embassy or consulate and pay a visa fee. You may be required to send in your passport and a picture to the embassy; the visa will be attached to a passport page and mailed back to you.

Certain countries require that you have proof of vaccinations upon entry into the country. The most popular one required is the yellow fever vaccination, particularly if you are coming from a country known to have yellow fever (this does not include the United States). The Centers for Disease Control and Prevention (CDC) and World Health Organization (WHO) offer vaccination recommendations and guidelines for certain countries. To obtain travel vaccinations, you may need to visit a travel clinic because primary care physician offices do not routinely carry travel vaccinations (yellow fever, typhoid). You may also need prophylactic medications for malaria, which can be prescribed by any physician.

When traveling internationally, always know where the US Embassy or consulate is in your destination city. You can contact them if you lose your passport (in case this happens, always have a copy of your passport on you, paper, or on your phone), need help to find local medical services, need medical evacuation, or unrest and danger occurs in the country. By registering with the Smart Traveler Enrollment Program (STEP) through the US State department (step.state.gov), you will:

1. Receive important information from the Embassy about safety conditions in your destination country, helping you make informed decisions about your travel plans.

2. Help the US Embassy contact you in an emergency, whether natural disaster, civil unrest, or family emergency.

3. Help family and friends get in touch with you in an emergency.

Before you leave home, make a copy of your passport and all of your credit cards to leave with a trusted person in the US. Once again, a copy of your passport (paper or on the smartphone) will be useful if lost or stolen.

UNDERSTANDING FOREIGN CULTURES

Before you visit an unknown city or country, research its culture. Read about normal customs, food, dress, and language. Learn a few phrases that will be useful: hello, goodbye, how much is this?, where is the bathroom?, where is the train?, etc. There are also smartphone apps such as Google Translate and Babbel to help you communicate.

Try to blend in with the environment as best as you can to exhibit an interest in their lifestyle. For instance, when I am in Paris I try to dress like a local and a tourist. I wear black pants or a skirt, flat walking shoes (no tennis shoes or baseball caps or named sweatshirts), sedate clothing, a neck scarf, and a cross-body bag. Always be respectful of the cultures and ways of living: never mock, ridicule, or ignore customs. Simply ask if you don't know.

ELECTRONICS

Phone service is available across the world. Check with your cellular carrier prior to leaving home about an international plan and roaming charges. Even text messages are charged an extra fee. The best solution is to place your cell phone in airplane mode and do not return to cellular service until you land back in the US except in an emergency. Most hotels, restaurants, and public areas internationally have Wi-Fi. You can receive text messages and email while on Wi-Fi, even if your phone is in airplane mode. If you are a buying customer, ask the staff of a restaurant or store for the Wi-Fi login. However, beware of "public" Wi-Fi where you are required to register and give personal information. Protect your identity.

Electrical outlets vary across the world. You need to carry an electrical outlet converter, which can switch from country to country. Also, bring with you a three-prong adapter in case your converter only accepts two prongs. These can be purchased online or at any discount store.

HOTEL AND LODGINGS

International hotels require you to show your passport upon check-in. They will make a copy of it to put on file: it's for the hotel security but may also help should you lose your passport.

Once you get in the room, you may be required to put the room card key in a slot at the door to turn on the electricity in the room. In some developing countries, electricity is fragile; take a flashlight in case of a power grid failure and keep the flashlight next to the bedside.

CURRENCY

Always know the currency of the country you are visiting. European countries have made it simple by all accepting Euros. Other countries may accept Euros, but additionally have individual currencies. Do not assume that the US dollar is accepted everywhere. The daily exchange rate of the US dollar to other currencies is published at exchange counters, airport, online, hotel front desk, and yes, there is an app for currency exchange.

Depending on the exchange rate, you can change your money before you leave the US or when you arrive in the destination country. I typically have a small amount of the local currency for when I land for food, taxi, and tips; and prefer to exchange the remainder in the country of my destination. The airport exchange centers generally will give you the lowest exchange rate. However, if you purchase foreign money in the US, you are guaranteed the ability to return and exchange unused money back into US dollars with your receipt. Most international cities that welcome tourists will also have exchange stores or counters within the city that may give you a better rate than at the airport or hotels. And sometimes, the hotel concierge can even direct you to the location that has the best exchange rate.

You can also purchase "cash" cards that work as a credit card with the local currency. You put a set amount on the card and it is reloadable. It protects you by not having to carry large amounts of cash and keeps you on budget. I always take two credit cards with me when I travel, but *never* my debit card. The credit cards are for any possible large purchases or an emergency (medical treatment, quick return flight, etc.). Before leaving home, alert your credit card company that you are traveling to another country and the dates of travel; you do not want them to stop your credit while traveling. If not alerted, they will see "unusual activity" out of the US and assume that your credit card was stolen or that you are a victim of fraud. Also verify with your credit card company if there are any transaction exchange fees; this is when you purchase an item in another country's currency and the credit card converts it into US dollars but charges a fee for the conversion.

CHAPTER 8

Swift Packing

Open your suitcase at least a week before you travel. As you think of items to take, drop them in the suitcase so they are available when you are ready to pack.

Some people promote Team Carry-On, meaning they *only* travel with a carry-on bag. But, if you are a first-time traveler, that task may be intimidating. I am

Team Carry-On when I travel for business, have a tight connecting schedule, or am going on a quick 1 to 3 day trip. I promote the one bag rule. Unless you are moving, staying at a destination for more than one month, or in a fashion show, you should be able to fit your clothes, shoes, or any necessities in one piece of luggage per person. This is important because, unless you are Elite status with an airline, you are required to pay for checked bags and you want to keep that cost to a minimum. The maximum weight of the checked bag is 50 pounds. You will also pay extra if it exceeds that weight. *Do not* pack the maximum weight because you won't leave any room for items you may obtain during your travels.

Here are my go-to tips for packing:

- Pre-plan your outfits for ease of packing. Choose clothes that are the basic blue, brown, and black so you can interchange for multiple looks.

- Wear your heaviest shoes or boots on the plane, preferably ones that easily come off during security.

- Three pair of shoes is sufficient for any travel: a comfortable walking shoe that may also double as your exercise shoe; a dress shoe (mine is usually a sandal that doubles as a dress shoe even in cold weather); and, depending on your activity, add a pair of fashion boots, hiking boots, or swim shoes. Flip flops are necessary for beach or shower wear, but those are easily packed in the outside pocket of your checked bag.

- Rolling your clothes saves space and reduces wrinkles.

- Compression bags and packing cubes compress the clothes and are space-efficient. I use the soft-side/mesh cubes for compacting clothes. Packing cubes are also efficient because, when I get to my destination, I just pull out a cube for an item without unpacking the entire suitcase.

- I use shoe bags to contain my shoes, but you can use a plastic bag for shoes to avoid dirtying your clothes. Or use the hotel plastic shower cap to cover the bottom of your dirty shoes.

- Socks and jewelry can be placed inside the shoes for space saving.

- Roll ties within the left-over cardboard tube from toilet tissue.

- When packing liquids in your checked luggage, place them inside a Ziploc bag in case of spills during the journey. It will not leak onto your clothes if it is sealed off.

- Use a contact lens case for liquid makeup instead of carrying the full bottle.

- When traveling internationally, take only your favorite must-have toiletries. Hotels often supply you with soap, shower gel, lotion, sewing kit, and shower cap. If you leave your toothbrush and toothpaste, most front desks will give you a kit. It may not be high quality but it will save you.

- Leave the expensive jewelry at home.

ITEMS TO CONSIDER PACKING

- Take a large shawl that works as a blanket on the airplane and a wrap for your dinner outings.

- Small face towels for international hotels: they typically do not supply smaller towels unless they are an US-owned hotel chain.

- Foldable bag: Bring this in your suitcase. You can fill it with any extra clothes or souvenirs that you may purchase and then check or carry it on your return flight.

- A mesh or plastic bag for dirty clothes: I place dryer sheets in my suitcase to keep it smelling fresh during my travels.

CARRY-ON BAGS

Your carry-on bag should only contain essential items necessary for the flight: valuable items and electronics, medications, keys, and anything you cannot live without if your luggage is lost. Pack an extra outfit/underwear in your carry-on in case the luggage does not arrive at the same time you do at your destination (yes, this happens sometimes). On my flight, I typically wear a comfortable pair of traveling pants (wrinkle-free, breathable material, dark to hide spots, and interchangeable with pockets), then pack an additional top to wear with the pants and a change of underwear in a Ziploc bag; just throw your used underwear in the bag when you change it.

I also include toothpaste, a toothbrush, facial wipes, small hand lotion, soap, deodorant, and lip balm in my carry-on. Travel size toiletries can be found in most stores. I carry a hand towel for various things, from taking care of spills to using it when I arrive at the hotel. Other items to consider in your carry-on: hand sanitizer, cleaning wipes, compression socks, snacks, eye masks, ear plugs, a flashlight, chargers, and an electrical outlet converter.

Remember, your carry-on must weigh 25 lbs./12 kg and be 21 inches long for US carriers or 19 inches for international carriers.

CHAPTER 9

Jet Lag

If you fly and change time zones more than three hours, you may experience jet lag. You land feeling sluggish and fatigued; this feeling may last up to 24 hours after landing. The change of time zones and extensive traveling throws off the circadian rhythm (your internal time clock) in your body for a while. You may avoid it by following these tips:

1. Get rest the night before. Do not stay up the night before packing or partying with the expectation of getting sleep on the airplane. You may not be able to sleep, or you may get stuck in a middle seat, or in a row with an active child or crying baby (it's not the baby's fault). Use ear plugs, noise-cancelling earphones, and an eye shade to help you sleep on the airplane. And a personal (not the reused ones that airlines offer) snuggling blanket to get comfortable rest. Lack of sleep can impair your brain's functions similar to being drunk; you want to be aware and functional when you reach your destination.

Transition your hourly clock a few days before you travel to the new time zone. At least 48 to 72 hours before your trip, try to function on the destination's time zone; gradual change of 2- to 3-hour difference. Once arriving at your destination, expose yourself to sunlight to help you adjust. Most flights that leave from the east coast to Europe leaves at night; you'll arrive at your destination between 6:00 am to 9:00 am. Most European hotels will accommodate the traveler and have some rooms available for early arrivals. You can always call the hotel 1 to 2 days prior to arrival to arrange for early arrival. When you land at your destination during the morning or daytime, do not go to sleep. If your hotel room is available, take a hot rejuvenating shower. If the room is not ready, store your luggage at your lodging, then hit the streets, and follow the local time. Have an early dinner and then bedtime.

2. Stay hydrated with water! Flying and travel will cause dehydration since your normal routine is changed. So, hydrate before you travel, during the flight, and after the flight. Yes, the water will cause you to go to the bathroom more, but it helps with the circulation in your legs and reduces the risk of blood clots. The true test of hydration is the color of your urine: clear and see-through means good hydration.

3. Eat light. Heavy foods, high carbohydrates and fried foods will cause fatigue and sleepiness. High sodium foods will cause water retention and leg swelling. In addition, gas-producing foods, including bubbly or carbonated drinks, expand in the pressurized airplane, causing abdominal bloating and discomfort. Avoid these foods at least 24 hours before the flight or else you may feel like you instantly gained ten pounds mid-flight.

Foods that can cause gas include: broccoli, cabbage, cauliflower, beans, lentils, apples, fluffy wheat, oats, onions, corn, potatoes, pears, peaches, milk, and soft cheese. Try to eat meals at the time of your destination.

4. Limit caffeinated and alcoholic beverages. These also contribute to dehydration.

5. Wear loose comfortable clothing. I wear clothes made of breathable material in case of sweating. Layer your clothing for on and off versatility due to climate changes and the cold airplane.

6. Walk and stay active to increase circulation. You should move every two hours while awake on the airplane. Once you get to your destination, be sure to take a 20-minute walk after eating a meal to maintain consistent digestive health and regularity.

CHAPTER 10

Eating While Traveling

EATING IN A DEVELOPING COUNTRY: BOIL IT, COOK IT, PEEL IT, OR FORGET IT!

You are no longer in the US and the Food and Drug Administration (FDA) guidelines regarding food preparation and storage no longer apply here. In many countries, you will find open air markets with the daily meats and produce on display without methods of preservation.

Unclean water and food can cause food poisoning and diarrhea but also other more serious diseases such as hepatitis A or typhoid. The CDC has an app called "Can I Eat This?" that you can download for free to help with your international journey.

Other points to keep in mind:

- Eat cooked food while it is hot. Avoid eating food that has been sitting out for a while.

- Eat fruits and vegetables only if you can peel them or wash them with clean water. Therefore, salads and salsa should be avoided.

- Avoid raw meat and "bush" meat (game meat of non-domesticated animals). The source of the meat is unknown and typically a wild animal; your body is not used to processing.

- Avoid raw or runny eggs.

- Use bottled water for drinking and cooking. Coffee and tea must be steaming hot before consumed. Tap water can be treated with chlorine or purification tablets or disinfected by boiling. Most 5- and 4-star hotels have water filtration systems but contact the staff to find out about their water sources.

- Drink only water, sodas, or sports drinks that are canned or bottled and sealed (carbonated is safer because the bubbles indicate that it was sealed at the factory). Avoid ice in drinks. They were most likely made with the local tap water.

- Pasteurized milk from a sealed bottle is fine but be careful of milk or cream sitting in an open container. People with compromised immune systems and pregnant women must avoid unpasteurized milk and dairy products (cheese, yogurts, etc.).

HEALTHY EATING AND DINING GUIDELINES: DOMESTIC, INTERNATIONAL, AND AT HOME

As a travel doctor who's always on the go, I frequently eat at airports, restaurants, and hotels. I have developed some eating habits to be conscious of the amount and types of foods I consume. These habits assist me in maintaining energy and good health. Let me share them:

1. Portion control: Be aware the size of your food portions per meal

   Protein: 3–4 oz.   Starches: ½ cup

   Vegetables: 1 cup   Sauces or dressing: ¼ cup

   - At a buffet, use a smaller plate (6-8 inches) to start. All the food should have its own space on the plate—do not pile it up! You can always go back for more.

   - Restaurants in the US typically serve 2–3 times the recommended meal portions. You can ask for the lunch portion size even during dinner hours. Many restaurants now list the caloric intake of each meal on the menu so preview it online to know their choices.

- Take half of your meal home with you and ask for a to-go box early.

2. Make substitutions: Some menus will specify "no substitutions" or "substitutions for an additional cost." An extra $1.50 for five pounds of less weight or a healthy heart is worth the cost.

- Sides: instead of fries, request grilled or fresh vegetables.

- Dressings: oil and vinegar, lemon, and balsamic are great replacements for high calorie creamy dressings. Be wary of low calorie or fat-free dressings: they may have a higher sugar amount to modify the taste.

- Only eat fresh salsa: must be made directly in the restaurant with fresh ingredients (avoid in developing countries).

- Be careful of "spreads" on sandwiches, since they can be high in calories, fat, and sugar. Consider replacing with mustards, relish, fresh vegetables, oil & vinegar, and spices.

- Go for whole wheat bread instead of white bread: multigrain is not 100 percent wheat.

3. Watch for add-ons such as croutons, bacon bits, "smothered with cream sauce," flavored butter, and cheeses.

   - Be careful of sauces and dressings. Restaurants usually drown foods in these add-ons, so ask for them on the side and you can add your own amount to the dish.

   - Be careful of sugar filled condiments.

4. Make a request: Order the meal the way you want it. Do not be intimidated by the server rushing you. Ask for what you want, whether its skinless chicken or breading removed from the meat. If it can't be removed, most likely it's a processed and packaged food filled with preservatives and added sodium.

   - Choose "Farm to Fresh" restaurants that use local farming products.

   - Alternative choices to fried: broiled, grilled, roasted, baked, steamed.

- Pizza: order thin-crust rather than stuffed, light on the cheese, and load with vegetables.

5. Drinks: Don't drink your calories! Water is an excellent choice for libation. Avoid the high-calorie, sugar-filled sodas or multiple refills of "specialty" drinks. If you need the bubbles or carbonation, try sparkling water, club soda, or seltzer water.

6. Timing: Try to eat at the same time each day. Your body is on a schedule for nutrients. Don't skip breakfast since it boosts your metabolism after a fast while sleeping.

   - Make it easier on yourself by pre-planning your meals.

   - Eat three full meals a day: breakfast, lunch, and dinner. Have low-calorie snacks such as veggies, fruit, and snack packs in between.

   - Avoid the hunger: hunger releases the hormone ghrelin, which will cause you to eat more. Eating every three to four hours will suppress ghrelin. Make reservations at the restaurant to avoid waiting to eat.

7. Don't over indulge and don't deprive yourself: choose healthy alternatives and food exchanges instead of starving and torturing yourself. Example: if you want dessert, consider skipping the mash potatoes in the main meal. When you deprive yourself, you increase the temptation to eat more.

8. Ways to avoid overeating

- Ask for a to-go box when the meal is served, divide it in half immediately, and pack away. You will not continue to nibble at the end.

- Place your fork down in between bites. Eat slowly and savor the flavor.

- Wait 20 minutes between dinner and dessert. It takes 20 minutes for your stomach to signal to your brain that it is full and satisfied.

- Share your meal with dining companions.

- Choose between appetizer and dessert, not both!

- Avoid bread or chips before the meal.

9. Watch your sodium intake: The recommended daily allowance of sodium for an adult is 2000 mg and even less for someone with hypertension, heart disease, or heart failure. Sodium will cause water retention, which results in swelling and bloating, an uncomfortable feeling after a day of flying or walking tours.

CHAPTER 11

How to Explore Your Destination

You made it, GREAT! Now, what to do?

Taxis from the airport are the not only mode of transportation; some taxi services within large cities have smartphone apps for service and to get estimated prices, i.e., London black taxi. However, modern day transportation options like Uber or Lyft may be more cost effective for travel within large cities. Ride-share shuttles are also available from airports but remember that you will make multiple stops so you cannot be in a hurry. Public transportation is always an option and can be culturally enlightening. Apps like Google Maps or Citymapper also let you know the schedules for trains and buses, and some cities like Paris have an app for their Metro, so that you can be informed about stops, connections, and real-time train times.

One of my go-to tours in most cities is the Hop On, Hop Off bus. It is available in US cities, Europe, and even Delhi, India. If you have not ever tried it, you need to do it at least once. It's a tour bus that travels around the city and stops at favorite tourist attractions while you listen to a recorded narrative tour, available in several languages (you can plug your earphones in to listen). The great part is that it allows you to get off the bus to explore the site, then get back on at the same stop or a different stop to continue the city tour. You can purchase tickets for one, two, or multiple days to use the bus. I use it often as my transportation around a city to the tourist sites. I also like to use public transportation around the city to immerse myself in the daily life culture.

You can find tours and activities at your destination through various means. You can consult your hotel concierge, public pamphlets, online sites such as TripAdvisor and Viator.com, travel agent recommendations, and more. Tour books to popular cities include detailed information about attractions, must-see sites, navigation, maps, transportation, restaurants, and the local social scene. These can be purchased online, in a bookstore, at airport travel store, or downloaded onto a tablet or phone. You can book some activities prior to travel or you can wait until you get to your location. Once again, research your destination to get the most out of your travel experience. Some popular tourist attraction will need advance reservation and payment, particularly if you are in the high season. For instance, you definitely want to get advance tickets to go up to the top of the Eiffel Tower; otherwise you may stand in line for 1 to 2 hours.

I also like to use the CityPass for popular cities, domestic and international. You pay a fee for a one to four-day pass and then get access to museums, tourist sites, skip the line, recorded tour headsets, transportation/metro tickets, the Hop On Hop Off bus tours; and coupons and discounts across the city. Plus, it comes with a guide book of the city. It is worth the investment for a comprehensive city tour.

Tour plans can keep you going every day and you try to fit in everything in one trip. In some cities, you can't see it all the first time; leave it for the anticipation to come back. Remember to add downtime to your sightseeing and adventures. You don't have to have every minute of the day occupied with an activity. If you are constantly going 12 hours a day on your vacation, you will come home exhausted and feel like you need another vacation. Listen to your body's clues for rest. Schedule quiet time if you are traveling with children. If you want to sleep in one morning, do it. Pamper yourself with room service breakfast and lounging in the bed. Choose a morning or afternoon to just walk the streets and people-watch. Be spontaneous to whatever you may find. Sometimes, no plan is the best plan.

CHAPTER 12

Traveling Healthy and Medical Problems Associated with Travel

Eating and drinking was discussed in a previous chapter. This chapter will supply tips and practices to stay healthy while traveling, and describe some common health problems related to travel.

THE BASICS OF HEALTHY TRAVEL

1. *Hydrate.* This is so important that I am repeating it. Flying will dehydrate you: the recycled air in the cabin, the altitude, the pressurized compartment, and changes in your daily routine all contribute to this fact. People also do not drink as much water before a flight because they don't want to get up and use the closet bathroom as often.

   However, hydration keeps your blood circulating, reduces risks of blood clots, reduces jet lag, and improves your overall health. You cannot bring liquids through airport security, but you can bring an empty bottle, reusable bottle/canister, or a collapsible travel bottle. Airports now have filling stations to fill the bottles with filtered water rather than you having to pay $2 to $5 per bottle.

2. *Boost your immune system.* Get enough sleep (6–8 hours each night). Do not stay up the night before you travel; you may not be able to sleep in the car, train, or plane as expected. If you have trouble sleeping, there are over-the-counter sleep-aids such as Melatonin; consult with your physician before taking extra medications and supplements.

Your immune system is affected severely by your stress levels. You can reduce your travel stress with adequate sleep, relax during delays by reading or an activity you enjoy, and nap in between tours. Also, take daily vitamins to complement your immune system.

3. *Keep your energy up.* Avoid foods with high sugar: these offer only temporary energy and will make you fatigued later. Protein snacks and nuts (if you don't have an allergy) are good afternoon sources of energy to keep you going while traversing the city.

4. *Wash your hands often.* Soap and water are the best way to prevent transmitting germs to yourself. You should use warm water and soapy suds to wash for at least 20 seconds. And make sure you get in between the fingers.

5. *Keep hand sanitizer and antiseptic wipes with you.* Hand sanitizer is the next best solution when soap and water are not available. Place it on both hands, rub them together, and allow them to air dry for 15 seconds. People transfer germs and viruses when their hands touch objects, and then they touch their faces. Viruses can live 8–12 hours on an object.

6. *Places to use antiseptic wipes*: airplane seat arm rests, seat buttons, screens, and tray tables; rental car steering wheels, gear shifts, knobs, buttons, door handles, keys and key fob; hotel room door handles, light switches, lamp switches, TV remotes, and telephones; baby-changing stations

TRAVELING WITH MEDICATIONS

Pre-travel medications for nausea, motion sickness, diarrhea, malaria, and other travel-related illnesses can be prescribed by your physician, a walk-in clinic, or a travel clinic. There are requirements for traveling internationally with prescribed medications, and some countries restrict certain drugs even if it is medically indicated.

Medications in foreign countries may be different, have a different name, come in different packing, and/or be written in an unknown language. It is best for you to travel with your prescribed medications and your favorite over-the-counter medications because you may not find them in the country of your destination. Your prescription medications should be in the original bottles with your name on the bottle and packed in the carry-on bag. Do not mix different types of pills in one bottle. If you are stopped by customs, your bottles may be inspected to verify the medication matches the label on the bottle.

Entering another country with unmarked medication can be considered drug trafficking, as is returning to the US with various unknown medications will be flagged as drug trafficking. The medications can be confiscated and destroyed, and you may be detained or even jailed. If you are carrying narcotics, sleep aids, anxiety medications or injectable medications, you should have a note from the prescribing physician on letterhead paper. Beware some countries do not allow you to bring controlled substances even if they have been prescribed.

MEDICAL TREATMENT IN A FOREIGN COUNTRY

Medical care in other countries may vary in quality and accessibility. You can check with the hotel concierge for a suitable medical facility, one that has English-speaking doctors. As mentioned previously, you will likely be expected to pay for your care with cash or a credit card. The US Embassy or consulate can help in obtaining the appropriate medical care while traveling and assist in evacuation if needed. If the US government evacuates you due medical reasons, you are still required to pay for the services.

If you have a chronic illness or are going on an adventurous trip, research of medical facilities and locations should be done in advance of your travel. Two resources to use are International Society of Travel Medicine (www.istm.org) or International Association of

Medical Assistance to Travelers (www.iamat.org). Plan by seeing your primary care physician before your trip for possible vaccinations or prophylactic medications for illnesses. Prepare for the climate, conditions, and possible environmental related health issues:

- Cold environment: take steps to avoid hypothermia and frostbite, rewarm immediately, and use room temperature water for rewarming extremities.

- High-altitude sickness: mild symptoms can start at 5000 feet (1500 meters) above sea level and mountain sickness at 8000 feet (2400 meters) above sea level. Know when to take medications and when to descend.

- Hot and sunny environments: avoid persistent sun exposure for hours, treat sunburns, stay hydrated to avoid heat illness, and wear lightweight breathable clothing.

TRAVEL-RELATED MEDICAL ILLNESSES

Blood clots: Deep Vein Thrombosis (DVT) and Pulmonary Emboli (PE)

When you travel (via car, train, or plane) for longer than four hours, you increase your risk of developing blood clots, also known as Deep Vein Thrombosis and Pulmonary Embolism (DVT/PE). Blood clots form when the veins in your legs are not moving for a long period of time. One leg may be more swollen than other (two to three times its normal size), skin that is hot to touch, calves that hurt to touch, redness, and pain with foot and toe movement or raising your toes. Blood clots may travel to your lungs. Blood clots in the lungs show up as chest pain, difficulty breathing or catching your breath. These are called pulmonary emboli (PE), a condition that will decrease your oxygen levels, strain your heart, and can cause death.

You are at increased risk for DVT/PE if you:

- Have had DVT/PE in the past

- Have had recent surgery (especially abdominal or orthopedic surgery)

- Are pregnant

- Are a smoker

- Are taking birth control pills or hormone replacement therapy

- Have cancer, restricted movement, or blood-clotting problems

- Have a family history of DVT/PE

- Are obese

- Have recently broken a bone

If you have any of these conditions, talk to your doctor before traveling. People at higher risk for DVT/PE may be prescribed medication during travel.

To prevent DVT/PE during flights:

1. Stay hydrated.

2. Wear loose-fitting clothing.

3. Walk around every two hours. Also, stretch your legs and arms at least once an hour. Pump your legs up and down, stretching the calves, and perform toe touches.

4. Wear compression socks or stockings that reduce leg swelling and encourage blood flow.

Traveler's diarrhea

One of the main reasons for dehydration in a traveler is diarrhea. Diarrhea is caused by eating food and/or drinking water contaminated with bacteria. Your gastrointestinal system is not immune to the local bacteria; therefore, you develop diarrhea and lose a large quantity of your body's water.

Many developing countries of the world do not have clean water sources. You may be in an area that uses a community water source from a river or lake. That water is not only used for drinking but also bathing, watering the animals, and washing clothes. You can easily be exposed to several bacteria and/or parasites. If you are unsure of the water source, use bottled water for drinking and cooking. Don't drink anything with ice in it; learn to drink room temperature drinks.

Contaminated water in developing countries also can affect your grooming, bathing, and swimming. Beware of cuts or open wounds, no matter how small, on your body; they must be covered and avoid contact with the water. This includes cuts you get while shaving that you then rinse with the water. Use filtered or bottled water to clean wounds, wash your face after shaving, and brushing your teeth. Do not swallow the water while taking a shower. Wear sandals or flip flops while taking a shower in case the drainage system is slow and the water pools on the shower floor. Parasites and worms can enter your body from the water through your feet. Do not swim in cloudy water. Some bacteria can be inhaled by steam or vapors in steam baths or while using a hookah.

Bug bites

Many diseases and parasites are carried by mosquitoes, ticks, fleas, and flies. Here is a very short list of what some bugs carry:

- Mosquitoes: dengue, chikungunya, malaria, Zika, yellow fever, Japanese encephalitis.

- Ticks: African tick-bite fever, Mediterranean spotted fever, tick-borne encephalitis.

- Others: scrub typhus (chiggers), plague (fleas), sleeping sickness (tsetse flies).

As mentioned in earlier, you may need pre-travel medications as disease prevention from these bites. They can be prescribed by your primary care physician, a walk-in clinic, a travel clinic, or telemedicine visits.

When traveling to an area that is known to have one or many of these diseases, wear insect repellent (natural-oil of lemon eucalyptus or chemical), particularly during the dusk and dawn periods. Adults can use an insect repellent that has DEET 20 percent or greater; children should not use DEET, but instead use natural insect repellent products. In addition, wear long sleeves and pants in areas where you might be exposed to insects. At night, sleep in a screened area with a net over your bed or sleeping bag. Unusual bug bites can also infect you with parasites.

If you develop a fever after a bite and the wound does not heal or you experience generalized illness, see a physician as soon as possible. If you have returned to the US, inform your medical provider of the country to which you traveled. Malaria may not show up for one (1) year after infected.

Sunburns

A sunburn is considered a first or second-degree burn from the sun. While you should always use sunscreen as protection, you must also limit your time of exposure to UV rays. Water, snow, and sand can intensify the sun rays, which means that the beach is not the only place you get sun exposure; hiking, skiing, mountain climbing, or being anywhere within the equator belt. While in the equator belt (between the Tropic of Cancer and Tropic of Capricorn), you can burn within 20 minutes of exposure since you are closest to the sun. In general, avoid direct exposure between 10:00 am to 2:00 pm.

Sunscreen should be applied at least 20 minutes prior to the exposure; this is how long it takes for it to be absorbed into the skin cells. Use a broad-spectrum UVA/UVB sunscreen with 30 SPF or higher. Reapply every two hours or after you've been in the water. Remember to put it on the top of your head, face, ears, and back of the neck. Lips should also be protected with a lip balm SPF 15 or greater.

Motion sickness

This condition occurs when your visual movement does not agree with the senses in your brain. You become dizzy, nauseated, and off-balanced, and sometimes, you will vomit. Motion sickness can occur with any form of travel.

In a car, sit in the front seat and focus on the horizon. On an airplane, sit over the wings. On a boat, sit at the center. Aromatherapy oils such as mint and lavender are helpful, as are ginger candies to calm the nausea.

If you are prone to having severe motion sickness or have had it before, contact your doctor for medication. If you plan to be on a boat for more than three days, patches are available for a steady infusion of medications. Keep in mind that some of these medications have side effects such as sleepiness and drowsiness.

MEDICATIONS TO TAKE WHILE TRAVELING

- Pain and fever relief

- Anti-diarrhea

- Motion or sea sickness

- Altitude sickness

- Antihistamine or allergy

- Anti-acid

- Decongestant

- Cough drops or cough suppressant (non-liquid)

- Laxative

PREVENTATIVE ITEMS

- Mosquito or insect repellant

- Hand sanitizer and wipes

- Antiseptic wipes

- Sunscreen

- Aloe

- Water purification tablets

FIRST AID

- Hydrocortisone or allergy cream
- Antiseptic wound cleanser
- Antibacterial ointment
- Aloe
- Eye drops
- Band aids
- Elastic bandage or ace wrap
- Oral rehydration tablets/salts
- Disposable gloves

CHAPTER 13

Safety While Traveling

MOTOR VEHICLE ACCIDENTS ARE THE NUMBER ONE CAUSE OF DEATH FOR TRAVELERS.

If you are driving a car or motorbike in a foreign country, beware of the laws and driving hazards. The roads may not be as maintained as in the US and many countries do not have marked lanes on their roads and highways, which only become more treacherous up mountains and around curves.

If you are in an accident, the emergency response and care may not be as adequate as in the US The US trauma system responds to the Golden Hour (1st hour after a trauma) to decrease the risk of mortality; in another country, you may still be lying on the side of a road or down a ravine during that Golden Hour. International EMS systems are not created equal to the US system.

To travel safely on the roads, avoid crowded, top heavy buses, don't drive at night in developing countries, and always wear your seatbelt or a helmet for motorbikes. Additionally, boating accidents may occur, which mix trauma and water injury.

BEWARE OF ANIMALS IN FOREIGN COUNTRIES.

A scratch or bite can carry many diseases. If such an incident occurs, wash the wound immediately with clean water and soap. Contact a physician as soon as possible. Rabies is transferred in the saliva of an animal via a bite or lick. If rabies is suspected, you must receive treatment as soon as possible. Rabies can be fatal, and the treatment may not be available in all countries as in the US. Rabies is typically found in dogs but can also be carried by bats. Bat bites are so small you may not notice that you've gotten one; if you wake up and there is a bat in your room, seek a healthcare professional just in case.

WEAR MINIMAL JEWELRY TO BE AVOID BECOMING THE TARGET OF A CRIME AND LEAVE THE EXPENSIVE JEWELRY AT HOME.

You will not wear it all the time and will have to worry about locking it in a safe wherever you go; remember that security is not always guaranteed. In most international countries and tourist sites, pick-pocketing is the biggest crime. If you must bring nice jewelry or valuables, use the front desk security deposit box.

STAY ALERT WHILE OUT ON THE STREETS.

Here are several quick tips to keep in mind when you're roaming around the city, especially in foreign countries:

- Don't drive with your hand out of the car while wearing a watch.

- Don't keep your wallet in your back pocket or backpack facing backwards.

- Use a cross body bag or purse, especially one with reinforced steel straps that can't be cut. People will drive past you on a moped, slash, and go. Check travel stores and online for security reinforced items. Some people wear passport holders around the neck, but I'd suggest against this: it signals that you are a tourist, thus, easy bait.

- Only get in marked taxis or car services.

- Be alert when walking across the street.

- Take a business card from the hotel before you leave for your activities. In case you need help getting back, you have the hotel's name, address, and phone number. If you don't speak the language of the city you are in, simply show the driver the card to get back.

HOTEL AND LODGING SAFETY

Always keep these points in mind while staying at a hotel or any other lodging, whether you are traveling domestic or international.

Lock your door each time you enter the room and use the dead bolt.

Check locks on windows, adjoining rooms, and balcony doors.

- Make sure hallways and parking structures are well lit.

- Request rooms between floors 3–6 (maximum height of fire department ladders).

- Don't have the front desk announce your room number when you check in.

- Sign the register with only your first initial and last name to keep your gender unknown.

- If you are a woman and traveling solo, book the room as two staying guests so it appears as if you are traveling with someone else.

- Make sure the credit card you use is the same one returned to you.

- Board the elevator last and select your floor button last. If you feel uncomfortable with the others, don't get on or get off on another floor than your own.

- Check the best escape route: find the location of the nearest stairwell and escape exit.

- Keep a flashlight, your room key, and your cell phone at your bedside

- Don't allow unannounced staff into your room: call the front desk to verify.

- Do not carry the hotel key in the card folder with the room number on it.

- Leave the "Do Not Disturb" sign on the door. Tell housekeeping to keep it on once they clean the room; if possible, leave the television turned on regardless of whether or not you are in the room.

CHAPTER 14

End of Vacation and Post Travel Illnesses

END OF VACATION

Now it's time to return home from your escape of daily life. Here are some things to remember at the end of your vacation:

- Use the folded extra bags you packed for souvenirs, extra items purchased, or dirty clothes (hopefully, you wore everything you packed, because you packed lightly!).

- Make sure once again that all liquids over 3.4 oz. are in a checked bag, including the free toiletries. This includes any alcohol purchased. You can buy bubble containers shaped like bottles to protect your purchases, or you can put them in a bag and wrap them in the dirty clothes. If the bottle breaks, the bag will contain the spillage.

- If you rented a car at the airport, please give yourself ample time (an extra 30–45 minutes) to return the car and take the shuttle or walk to the terminal.

- Review your pre-travel checklist and the list of things you brought with you to ensure that you are not forgetting anything.

- Reflect and record/write something about your trip, perhaps your favorite moment or meal or about something you learned along the way. There's always social media for you to keep track of your journey.

- Say farewell, not goodbye.

POST-TRAVEL ILLNESS

If you get sick after your travels, see a medical provider as soon as possible. Let them know when you traveled, where you traveled, and if anything occurred (injury, insect bite, weird foods eaten, body fluid exposures, medical procedures through medical tourism, tattoos, or piercing). Your physician can alter the examination and tests according to the diseases you might have been exposed to and can also search for unusual sources of the illness.

POSSIBLE POST-TRAVEL SYMPTOMS

These are the most common conditions that travelers experience when returning home.

- Diarrhea: We talked about traveler's diarrhea before. However, if you have persistent diarrhea (10 or more stools in a day or diarrhea lasting more than two days), we want to discover the source and treat accordingly.

  Common bacteria that causes diarrhea are E. coli (different types), giardia, shigella, or vibrio. Each bacterium presents differently so doctors will want to know about your stool. What color is it? Does it have a smell? Is there blood, mucous, or a greasy appearance? Is it loose, runny, or watery? Do you have abdominal cramping, gas, or bloating? Most likely, you'll be asked to provide a stool sample for testing. Your doctor will then prescribe you the right medication to treat the bacteria or, in some cases, worms and parasites from water sources that also cause diarrhea.

Persistent diarrhea can cause obstruction of the intestine and/or dehydration, since the intestines are pulling water out of your tissues and blood, attempting to wash out the bacteria. Accompanying symptoms may include nausea, vomiting, loss of appetite, headache, and fatigue. Children and the elderly are more at risk for severe dehydration that may require hospitalization. To avoid dehydration with diarrhea, drink 8 ounces of water every time you have a bowel movement.

- Fever: a fever is a common symptom in many illnesses. However, a fever is most concerning when you have been traveling in the equator belt (between Tropic of Cancer and Tropic of Capricorn). Countries within the belt are known for viruses carried by mosquitoes: malaria, yellow fever, Dengue fever, chikungunya, and Zika. Malaria, for instance, manifests as high fevers, chills, rigors, and severe headache; plus, it's cyclic, meaning you will get sick, get better, and then, two weeks later, get sick again.

Some forms of malaria have a medication resistance, so your doctor will need to know the specific country you visited. Then, they will diagnose you based on whether they find malaria in your red blood cells. Preventive anti-malaria medications are available from medical providers, so take it prior to the trip, during the trip, and after the trip.

- Blood clots: We discussed this extensively earlier. Blood clots occur when your blood is thick and stagnant in place for a long period. To reduce the risk, hydration is very important; it keeps your blood flowing. Walk every 2 hours on long trips; exercise your legs and calves. While sitting, perform toe touches/tip toe crunches, move your foot up and down, and march in place. If you suspect that you have blood clots, go to your physician or the nearest emergency department. An ultrasound of your legs and a CT scan of your chest are necessary to rule out blood clots.

- Dehydration: When dehydrated, you may experience symptoms such as muscle aches, soreness, joint pain, fatigue, and possibly fever. In severe cases, it will lead to rhabdomyolysis: your muscles break down and the resulting product (lactic acid) is a large molecule that gets stuck in your kidneys and causes kidney failure. You will require a large amount of fluids intravenously for rehydration and may require hospitalization.

- Rash: you may develop a rash from exposure to different plants and vegetation, your clothes being washed in a foreign country's water and detergent, bug bites, and various other scenarios. Inform your medical provider of the country you visited and possible things you came in contact with such as bugs or chemicals.

- Sunburn: As discussed in a previous chapter, a sunburn is a true burn. A first-degree burn causes extreme redness and a second-degree burn forms blisters. To treat a sunburn, stay out of the sun for a few days, apply cool compresses on the affected area, take cold showers, get lots of fluids, take pain relievers if necessary, and apply aloe to keep the burned skin moisturized. If you must go in the sun, cover the sunburned skin properly. If a large surface area of your body is sunburned, you can develop sun toxicity or poisoning. Along with the blistering skin, you will experience swelling, tingling, headache, fever, nausea, dehydration, and dizziness. If this occurs, seek medical treatment as soon as possible.

Epilogue

In this book, I focused mainly on topics regarding air travel and international travel. I only touched some main points so that you could get more comfortable with getting off the couch and booking an awesome vacation. I have much more to share about traveling, from navigating my favorite city, Paris, as an first time traveler and exploring the United States to cruising and more. Stay updated about volumes of *Travelpedia* to come by following me on all social media @YvetteMcQueenMD and browsing my website at www.yvettemcqueenmd.com.

Ciao and Travel Well!

Follow the links to obtain your travel products

Collapsible Travel Water Bottle:

https://mcqueenmd.samcart.com/products/travel-water-bottle

Travel First Aid Kit:

https://mcqueenmd.samcart.com/products/travel-first-aid-kit

Travel First Aid Kit with Medications:

https://mcqueenmd.samcart.com/products/travel-first-aid-kit-with-medications

Luggage Grip:

https://mcqueenmd.samcart.com/products/luggage-grip

Appendix:

TSA SCREENING OF BABY FORMULA/ MILK/FOOD, MEDICATIONS, & SPECIAL CONDITIONS

Screening Formula, Breast Milk and Juice[1]

TSA officers may need to test liquids for explosives or concealed prohibited items. Officers may ask you to open the container and/or have you transfer a small quantity of the liquid to a separate empty container or dispose of a small quantity, if feasible.

Inform the TSA officer if you do not want the formula, breast milk and/or juice to be X-rayed or opened. Additional steps will be taken to clear the liquid and you or the traveling guardian will undergo additional screening procedures, to include a pat-down and screening of other carry-on property.

X-ray Screening

The Food and Drug Administration states that there are no known adverse effects from eating food, drinking beverages, and using medicine screened by X-ray.

---

1 "TSA: Traveling with Children." *TSA | Transportation Security Administration | US Department of Homeland Security*, www.tsa.gov/travelers/airtravel/prohibited/permitted-prohibited-items.shtm.

3-1-1 Liquids Rule Exemption

Formula, breast milk, and juice in quantities greater than 3.4 ounces or 100 milliliters are allowed in carry-on baggage and do not need to fit within a quart-sized bag. Remove these items from your carry-on bag to be screened separately from the rest of your belongings. You do not need to travel with your child to bring breast milk.

Ice packs, freezer packs, frozen gel packs, and other accessories required to cool formula, breast milk, and juice are allowed in carry-on. If these accessories are partially frozen or slushy, they are subject to the same screening as described above. You may also bring gel or liquid-filled teethers, canned, jarred, and processed baby food in carry-on baggage. These items may be subject to additional screening.

Medications[2]

Medications in pill or other solid form must undergo security screening. It is recommended that medication be clearly labeled to facilitate the screening process. Check with state laws regarding prescription medication labels.

You are responsible for displaying, handling, and repacking the medication when screening is required.

---

2 "TSA: Disabilities and Medical Conditions." *TSA | Transportation Security Administration | US Department of Homeland Security*, www.tsa.gov/travelers/airtravel/prohibited/permitted-prohibited-items.shtm.

Medication can undergo a visual or X-ray screening and may be tested for traces of explosives.

Inform the TSA officer that you have medically necessary liquids and/or medications and separate them from other belongings before screening begins. Also declare accessories associated with your liquid medication such as freezer packs, IV bags, pumps, and syringes. Labeling these items can help facilitate the screening process.

You may bring medically necessary liquids, medications, and creams in excess of 3.4 ounces or 100 milliliters in your carry-on bag. Remove them from your carry-on bag to be screened separately from the rest of your belongings. You are not required to place your liquid medication in a plastic zip-top bag. If a liquid, gel, or aerosol declared as medically-necessary alarms, then it may require additional screening and may not be allowed

- Accessories: Ice packs, freezer packs, gel packs, and other accessories may be presented at the screening checkpoint in a frozen or partially-frozen state to keep medically necessary items cool. All items, including supplies associated with medically necessary liquids such as IV bags, pumps, and syringes must be screened before they will be permitted into the secure area of the airport.

- Screening: TSA officers may test liquids, gels, or aerosols for explosives or concealed prohibited items. If officers are unable to use X-ray to clear these items, they may ask to open the container and transfer the content to a separate empty container or dispose of a small quantity of the content, if feasible.

Inform the TSA officer if you do not want your liquid medication to be screened by X-ray or opened. Additional steps will be taken to clear the liquid and you will undergo additional screening procedures to include a pat-down and screening of other carry-on property.

References

ONLINE SITES FOR AIRFARE ALERTS AND DEALS

www.airfarewatchdog.com

www.farecompare.com

www.theflightdeal.com

www.skyscanner.com

www.flighthub.com

www.google.com/flights

www.kayak.com

www.faredeals.com

www.cheaptickets.com

www.secretflying.com

www.faredealalert.com

www.lookupfare.com

POPULAR TRAVEL ONLINE SITES:

www.expedia.com

www.priceline.com

www.hotwire.com

www.groupon.com
[vacation packages]

www.lastminutetravel.com

www.hotels.com

www.travelzoo.com

www.orbitz.com

www.travelocity.com

www.vacationstogo.com

www.onetravel.com
 [last minute deals]

www.trivago.com

www.booking.com

www.travelpirates.com

*** and many more and new each day

TRAVEL APPS (A FEW):

- Gate Guru: Map of terminals, review of food in airports, wait time of security checkpoints, etc.

- Entrain or JetLag Genie: Adapt circadian cycle for time zone changes

- WhatsApp: Text messaging system cross-platforms

- Hotel Tonight: Last minute room rates

- Maps.me: Offline mobile maps

- Google Translate

- Weather

- Viator

- Opentable or Forks: Restaurants and reservations

- TripIt or Worldmate: Store all your travel details in one space

- Foursquare

- Onanda Currency Converter or Currency +

- Lounge Buddy: Airport lounges, access, and reviews

- Babbel

- Airbnb

- Citymapper

- Google Maps

- Gas Buddy

- Goby: Event finder

- CDC: Can I Eat This?

- Time Out

- Mobile Passport

Quick Tips

- Leave room for spontaneity.

- Confirm all reservations, bookings, and prices prior to leaving home.

- Check the airline for delays or cancellations: downloading the apps will be helpful.

- Get medical travel insurance for international trips: add the evacuation portion.

- Stay hydrated to avoid jet lag.

- Have protein snacks for long trips. Avoid high-sodium, processed foods that cause swelling and high-sugar foods that give you temporary energy.

- Wear support (compression) socks or hose while traveling via airplane and walking.

- When buying a vacation package, make sure it includes the transfer from plane/train to your lodging and other travel needs.

- Wear socks or slip-on footies to avoid cold, dirty floors when going through TSA.

- Arrive at the airport an extra 30–45 minutes early when dropping off a rental car so that you have enough time to take the shuttle or walk back to the terminal.

- Carry-on bags should only weight 25 lbs./12 kg.

- Exfoliate and hydrate during travel.

- Use the airline app to choose or change seats and check for delays or cancellations.

- Notify your credit card companies of international travel and dates.

- Take a business card from the hotel before you leave for your activities.

- Reduce travel stress by sleeping and getting rest before your trip.

- Have extra activities planned in case there are any delays.

- Rest or take naps in between tours or before a night out on the town.

- Use your memberships, schools, or clubs for traveling discounts.

Vacation Planner

Destination: _____

Dates: _____

Number of people: _____

Flight: purchase at least 21 days before travel dates

Airport Parking: _____

Flight reservation and flight #: _____

Time of Departure: _____

Seat Selection: _____

Time between connecting flights:

Time of arrival:_____

Transfer to lodging: _____

Car Rental Company: _____

Reservation #:_____

Type of car: _____

Fuel charge: _____

Insurance or waiver: _____

Hotel/Rental/Airbnb Reservation #: _____

Deposit amount: _____

Return flight date: _____

Time of Departure: _____

Flight #: _____

Seat Selection: _____

Time of Arrival: _____

PRE-FLIGHT TO-DO LIST:

1. Check your flight status and your seats. Make sure they are the ones you originally chose (sometimes, the aircraft changes), look for better seats, or upgrade to Comfort class.

2. Drink plenty of water two to three days prior to your flight.

3. Avoid gaseous foods such as broccoli, cabbage, cauliflower, carbonated beverages, etc.

4. Pick up some compression socks to wear on long flights.

5. If traveling internationally,

   a. Call your credit card companies to tell them about the countries you are visiting and the days you will be traveling.

   b. Make a copy of a passport.

   c. Bring an electric converter and charge all your electronics before leaving home.

6. Check the weather and conditions of your destination.

7. Unplug your appliances at home.

8. Bring hand sanitizers and wipes.

About the Author

Yvette McQueen, MD, is an Emergency Medicine physician, travel doctor, instructor, speaker, entrepreneur, author, and consultant. She has traveled to over thirty countries worldwide, serving both travelers and local residents, promoting health education, travel wellness, and disease prevention. Over the years, she has organized medical missions to Africa, performed hospital training and teaching in Rwanda and Tanzania, conducted wilderness emergency care training and international teaching for the American Heart Association, and participated in international church missions.

Dr. McQueen is the CEO of MedQueen LLC, through which she offers travel medicine, urgent care, and nutritional consultations via telemedicine to individuals, executives, and travel groups. As a locum tenens physician, she also travels across the United States, providing her services in hospitals' emergency departments.

Dr. McQueen obtained her medical degree from Medical College of Ohio in Toledo and completed her Emergency Medicine residency in Detroit, Michigan. She currently resides in Jacksonville, Florida.

To connect, visit her website at
www.yvettemcqueenmd.com

CREATING DISTINCTIVE BOOKS
WITH INTENTIONAL RESULTS

We're a collaborative group of creative masterminds with a mission to produce high-quality books to position you for monumental success in the marketplace.

Our professional team of writers, editors, designers, and marketing strategists work closely together to ensure that every detail of your book is a clear representation of the message in your writing.

Want to know more?
Write to us at info@publishyourgift.com
or call (888) 949-6228

Discover great books, exclusive offers, and more at
www.PublishYourGift.com

Connect with us on social media

@publishyourgift

CPSIA information can be obtained
at www.ICGtesting.com
Printed in the USA
JSHW021342201219
3071JS00004B/7